Str(

The Second Canadian Poetry Association Anthology

Sheila Hyland, Editor

Broken Jaw Press
Fredericton • Canada

Strong Winds

Printed and bound in Canada by Sentinel Printing, Yarmouth NS.

Canadian Cataloguing in Publication Data
Main entry under title:

Strong Winds

     ISBN 0-921411-60-X

1. Canadian Poetry (English) — 20th century. * I. Hyland, Sheila.
II. Canadian Poetry Association.

PS8279.S87 1997   C811'.5408   C97-950141-5
PR9195.7.S87 1997

Broken Jaw Press
the literary imprint of
MARITIMES ARTS PROJECTS PRODUCTIONS
Box 596 Stn A
Fredericton NB E3B 5A6   ph/fax 506 454-5127
Canada   e-mail: jblades@nbnet.nb.ca

Strong Winds

The Second Canadian Poetry Association Anthology

Introduction

This second anthology by a diverse group of writers, all members of the Canadian Poetry Association, brings you variety of subject and style. Some names you will recognize, others will be less familiar. Among the prize-winning poets, I am happy to include Raymond Souster, famous for poems on everyday happenings. A Life Member of the CPA, Raymond Souster won the Governor General's Award for Poetry (1964) and received the Order of Canada (1995).

I was struck by the many love poems submitted for the anthology. This delighted me, as I took it to mean that despite our existing socio-economic depression, Canadians can still relate to one another and communicate their feelings.

Included here are Canadian authors from various originating countries including: East Germany, England, Guyana, Latvia, Wales, The Netherlands and USA. Submissions from members living abroad came directly from England and Malta.

Strong Winds is named from a poem by Dorothy Livesay (1909-96). "From the husk of the old world / To the new I fly / Strong winds beating / In a bluer sky". Livesay twice won the Governor General's Literary Award for Poetry (1944 and 1947) along with many other prizes. She produced numerous books, was a literary editor/publisher and an advocate of People's Poetry. Continuing the People's tradition, this anthology presents both positive and negative aspects of life. Alongside poems on ecstacy and beauty you will find some on poverty and streetlife. The poets in *Strong Winds* write with empathy and humour about love, loss, fear, courage, and every imaginable topic. Many poems for many people. Enjoy!

Grateful thanks to Joe Connor and Chris Roberts who very generously offered me use of their computer to put this manuscript on disk. Thanks also to Allan Briesmaster for proofreading.

— Sheila Hyland
June, 1997

Becky Alexander

Poetry

Poetry drops
in gelatinous blobs
spreads outward:
multiple concentric ripples,
searching muddied waters.

Rushing through
minds, blowing
with colours more
vibrant than red,
it blasts open windows
and slams doors.

Leaves you
refreshed —
a mint tang
of aftertaste,
tempting you back
to the beginning;
or,
stunned with the pain
of a grab at your throat —
makes you wish you
never knew the end
which now sticks
like a thorn
in the paw.

Poetry may not be easily digested,
but it makes me hungry.

Claire Alexander

Sudden Winter Wonderland

Black trunks spire ever higher
Towering through a blaze-like fire.

Early snows come softly falling
As the jays are screeching, brawling,
And the cardinal is calling.

Liquid shadows slipping, dripping
Through the snowbanks whipping, dipping.

Something comes out snooping, stalking
And the trees are whisper-talking.

After a painting of the same name by Joyce Hollowell shown June 1996 at Mill
Pond Art Gallery, Richmond Hill, Ontario.

Judith Anderson Stuart

What the Mushroom-Pickers Found

This stinking mass,
disintegrating flesh and bone,
inseparable
from the poor cloth and earth around it —
this clotted heap
tells two stories.

To investigators,
officially bristling
with meters and measurements:
a female, early twenties,
death from strangulation and/or
blunt blow to cranium.
Dated (by generations of maggot life)
Fall /86.

To the family:
O God!
our daughter —

Beryl Baigent

Waiting For The Azure Sister

> *Wild Spirit, which art moving everywhere;*
> *Destroyer and preserver; hear, oh, hear.*
> — Shelley

May I be a hollow bone
  standing nakedly facing sunset.
May I relinquish and release
  be like falling leaves with no regrets.
May I elicit my elder nature
  and assimilate by opening my heart.
May I experience the Dragon
  whose eyes flash   whose voice is thunder.

May I be purged of contamination
  by the west wind and internal lightning.
May I become a waving cloud and let my mind
  drop below the horizon of consciousness
  below intellect and discrimination
  to the still, greening centre.

And from this enclosure of bone and blessing
  by the binding of wind and thunder
  let my legacy be born   to balance the world.

★The title is a reference to Shelley's "Ode to the West Wind" in which Spring, as in
Taoism, is rebirth.

Winona Baker

Haiku Seasonal

old pond —
frog's eggs float
in my reflection

a dragonfly
was on the lily pad
before that swallow

it's happened:
my mother doesn't know me —
first autumn rain

high rise shadow
falls on the cardboard box —
vagrant's winter home

a dark path
in the white cemetery
ends in a snowman

Joachim (Jack) Baum

Lost Without You

When you are away
    I am so desperately lost,
as the sun on a cloudy day;
    or when the heavens play host
to clouds, hiding stars and moon,
    I am lost.
    But my innermost
feelings are so very fey
they calm when you are with me again.

George I. Bernstein

The Singer And The Song

All the music I hear
I hear through your voice
and the notes that are
missing
the notes I cannot hear
are carried to me
on the wings of your beauty

You are the gardener
who in the winter of my life
plants spring flowers
in the garden
of my soul

The irreversibility of time
Ends my impossible dream

Joe Blades

Mona Lévi

Portrait with expression énigmatique
M(ad)ona sans child
No rallying flag over barricades
No lighting the dream harbour

You grace my pizza box
Artist supplies in your arms
holding secrets for millions
of strangers whom gaze upon

No one has pulled you apart
Horses whipped and straining
haven't torn your secret
your unseen red tab landscape

O Mona   all of us catch
ourselves in your smile —
that sign   that language
we lust without knowing

Beyond life you are recreated
poem and myth outside of time
recreated in us silent
performers   always here   smiling

Allan Briesmaster

North Shore Suite

Outside radio range
one   hears only eldest news:
wood tunes, quiet change.

Boggy tracks ... trudge towards
heartwoods where slow piccolos
run both scales and chords.

Quivering pristine rilles.
White ribbon; thinnest among all
the veils on these hills.

Superior, cold in July,
draining dark tone off the sky:
restless fog-plumed sea.

Swift mists   softly harrow
(as lichen, waves, ice, have smoothed)
that black lava-pillow.

Six flames the storms left.
Under sunny mist, wood lily
licks from basalt cleft.

Elemental malice
hacks that red bluff's face. Quick birch
swabs up: lightgreen talus.

Glow-window, shelved clouds
cool-golden, outlandish-distant
— embers near this tent.

M. Brissett

Let The Blow Fall

Let the blow fall, I expect it,
The inevitable hour;
Let it fall, I can't reject it
Or its final power;
I was born for such a moment,
While in this world I linger;
And when borrowed time is all spent,
And I'm hooked on death's finger,
I must then relinquish gladly
To the silent reaper
What was loaned; though perhaps sadly,
As I'm sinking deeper.

Let the blow fall now, tomorrow,
Next year, when it pleases;
I'm held hostage to its horror
As it smirks and teases.
Life's knife handle is in its keeping,
I, the blade, am holding;
Held captive, waking or sleeping,
Need I bother scolding?
I will live life and not languish,
Nor shall I be clinging
To gloom. If I have my last wish,
I will go out singing.

Evelyn Broy

A Woman's Cheek

How many times have I sat like this,
cheek on hand, deeply pondering?
Today my cheek rebels at other thoughts
and claims some thinking of its own.
O, it has known the heartbeats
in a husband's breast, and
his loving, curved hand;
and how many times
have I carried his hand
to my cheek, with love?
Now that he's gone, it knows the glass
in a photo-frame — but I thank God
my cheek has also known the silk
of a daughter's hair and the wandering
infant fingers of a son.
Lips and eyes are themes for
lovers' love of mystery,
but this, my cheek's a book
of secret history.

Mary Chryssoulakis

Canadian Metamorphosis

The slanting March sun
shines through the window
drawing me from my cocoon.

I creep outside in
furry caterpillar clothes.
With hollow hungry eyes
I rake dead leaves
to find the first
tender green shoots.

April rains slake
May suns nourish
my chrysalis days
until ...

Amid bright June flowers,
with rosy skin and
rainbow raiment,
I emerge ...

a slightly battered butterfly.

Barbara Coulston

Coolness

I bare
only my feet,
cool and milky
white
as
the rain falls,
the sweet smell
of
lighted spring
raw,
still,
as you whisper your
dream,
playfully
shadowing my
skin.

Dina E. Cox

Lovesong

We   who have had
these children
             together
shared moments of
passion and
remembrance.
That   was before
the years of confusion,
            grasping together
clinging
            asunder,
struggling to understand
this velcro convergence;
            still
I love you

Caroline H. Davidson

Neighbours

I tells 'er, I does
I says, You fence up them dogs
so's they don't dump their lumps
on my yard.

I can't be always pickin' up
their lumps when I's mowin'
this 'ere grass.

I wants me grass to look nice
an' it does!
But them pups leaves their lumps in it
makes me mad.

I tells 'er, I did.

James Deahl

Prayer for the Dead in September

All evening that bird
has called from his weeping beech,

now the Pleiades pierce the heart of Heaven,
welcome the pain of the first iron frost.

In flowing robes the sisters turn and
return across this harvest earth.

And the dead, so still in their lying down,
seem truly beyond words —

yet words ascend the transfiguring dark.
There are no good-byes,

only a scattering of prayer candles
and the thin grass awaiting

winter's Grace.

Luci Dilkus

Eleven

The spirit of Winter robs me of my breath
though Autumn's beauty an overwhelming sight
of death
victims of the wind crack and grind
a deafening noise like memories unforgiving

decay

> yet a simple shift of gaze from in to out
> where children laugh while trampling
> death beneath their feet
> an embryo exhales into my breast
> and nurtures me

Sonja Dunn

Ukraine Poem 1

The dampness of my dacha
in Ukraine's Vorzel's Forest
seeps into my bones
assaulting my pampered body
through the thin slab
of a too short mattress

How many Tee-shirts
does it take
to keep warm

That ancient Ukrainian moon
transparent like vodka
forces her way
through bars of
unscreened windows
she lays her head
on my pillow
and tells me
"Nothing is easy in Ukraine."

Bernadette Dyer

Stone Woman

She will not show her face
It is a solemn one
That hides behind a waterfall
Of tears.
Her trampled heart
Falls out windows,
Dying repeatedly from dawn until dusk,
And in the rare moments
Of your presence
Is reduced to rubble
For her granite stoic concerns dissolve
Into infinite excuses
For your absences,
The holes you leave in the air
Your dizzying minefield of obligations
As you work late in restaurants
Preparing lunches for Ottawa girls
Who thrive on cubed melon slices,
A Mayan vision, and meetings
That aid in editing out-takes from food bank rushes,
Films that freeze time against frames, against tears
As you analyze *Macbeth*, an intrigue of language
And *Henry the Fifth*, a seduction of your senses
Before relations from Banff
Arrive in Richmond Hill
To demand undivided attention,
While she, a statue waxen
Bleeds alone with candle incantations,
Smudge sticks, herbs,
And tumbled stones.

Bob Ezergailis

Planetary Asylum

Most of the world
population
has always been
completely insane,
as most of them
cannot distinguish
themselves
from others,
particularly self
from leaders
and ideologues
of many kinds,
and more so
the self
from brainwashing,
as it is all
always within
their own brain
circuitry.

Raymond Fenech

Life Passes You By

There's a time when shades in the mind grow deep,
When thoughts are like the dusting of dreams,
And life seems to have passed without ever having been;
This is what it's like, the way it seems to be,
A sudden rude awakening from a long, long sleep.

Man tries in vain to arrest the process of time,
It escapes, it passes him by, leaving no trace;
Except age, those wrinkles cutting deep in his face,
And youth, all aspirations, strength and breath
Come and go with the centuries and unavoidable death.

Penny L. Ferguson

Waiting for the School Bus

As I wait for my son
at the bus stop,
I watch her
swirling her foot,
drawing arcs in the snow.

Sunglasses hide
the pain in her eyes
but grief chokes her voice,
tugs at her lips
as she tells
the crossing guard
her father is dying.
After months of struggle
his body has given in
to the inevitability
of the cancer consuming him.

She has not yet told
her three children
Grampy is dying.
That will be done tonight
when their father is home.

From the fringe
I listen,
her grief spreading,
enveloping me
like a burial shroud
and I long to offer comfort
but, a stranger,
I resist intruding
on her pain.

Peggy Fletcher

Unnatural Disaster

Words crash like ocean waves
high tide of anger
buries everything
in its cold depths. We huddle
inert in shells, unable to escape
forces that flood the flesh.

A tidal wave of change
crushing in its wake,
remorseless in its power.

After the storm subsides,
we are shaken
by the sound of excuses
flowing across the room
shattering the silence.

Jennifer Footman

December Thaw

This is my December thaw. The just dead earth
responds to a strange untimely stimulus,
delivers summer in winter.

Path oozes under my feet,
mud rolls into my shoes. Sleepy frog
blinks and stares at me as if looking for a season.

Dry lilac bushes come to life,
tight buds open just enough for green to sing
while sap drops thick, heavy.

Squirrel plays hide and seek
in mossy grass islands
between diminishing banks.

I know winter has to come.
This is not the time for rotting snow,
but is candy-cane time, a false handle

to see me through dark months of penance.
Sentence must be served, intervals bridged.
If only I could duck

under the death-freeze, hide,
even if it did mean I missed the redwings,
I'd take the chance to keep

lilacs in bloom winter to winter.

Linda Frank

Silent Lover

She found a lover
who made no demands
who had no need to tell
and no need to ask
She never knew his name

She loved best
his silence
how he could keep still
in the belief
that there was no need
to know. He'd saved her
in his vacant room void
of light but for the dirty
yellow glow of the yawning fridge
that haloed his wares
There were no questions
In all their time
together, they spoke no more
than a few dozen words
She believed he knew her
thoughts by reading
what he stared at in her eyes

How could anyone lose desire
for a lover with an inner life?

She'd only wanted her emptiness
to be filled by his

Kathy Fretwell

Summer Hiatus

A receptive lotus, I wait.
Dazed from the assembly-line
I grab a towel and take a hike.

On my Walkman, Shostakovitch
leapfrogs percussion & brass over
my brain beached in the backyard.

The notes twitch, grass dances.
Strings and woodwinds toss melodies
in the breeze.

Then like a tidal wave
the full orchestra crests,
splashes my brain back into grooves.

Now my words roar, skid, do wheelies.

Edward Gates

XXV

the small stream   the fall rain
light gathers in the spaces between trees

breathe deep   there is no telling
how the spruce grow

wind moves   boards creak
there is warmth in an old blanket and knife

is that noise from a branch broken
by the foot of an old friend

quiet   the opening is not large
and the animals hear the smallest sounds

Ben Genereaux

Two little babies
Face down and floating
Feeling bloated and blue
Dancing in playtime fields
With teddy bears and Barbie dolls
Waiting for some salvation
Something old and out of reach

Two little babies
Mouths open and gasping
Feeling robbed and berated
You've come to our rescue
Please, just leave us here
Face down and floating
Feeling bloated and blue

Two little babies
Sold to slavery and rape
Living voids of death
Walk away and be thankful
Find some way to forgive us
Mouths open and gasping
Feeling robbed and berated

Katherine L. Gordon

Night of the Wolves

He sends me wolves.
I glimpse them waiting
With an awful stillness
On the edges of my path.
Their shaggy weight, wild-scented,
Presses on my bed at night
Their red wolf eyes flaring like binary stars
In the blackness of an unexplored space
Carry the message:
He is walking again between the worlds.
Everything in this neat and sanctified house
Blasphemes out of place
Chaos beneath the unctuous order of every church
Nothing can ever be ordinary again.
He sends for me, who am afraid to follow.
In the spiral dance
Of the long wolf night
The vortex waits.

Lini Richarda Grol

At The Special Olympics

Armless they struggle and swim
Against the strong current.
Fearless they climb a mountain
Expecting to reach the horizon
Which seems for ever receding.

Holding their breath
The mothers tremble and
Cringe when they see
How their children fight
Against life's cruel mishaps.

But the children
Ignoring their lack,
Are unaware of what others call
Their severe handicap, and
Bravely race for their goal.

Fighting the odds,
They shout and chant,
Do what they want,
And laughing out loud
They reach their Olympus.

Richard M. Grove

Breath of Content

Only as the waters calm to glass
with the stillness of wanting nothing
can one see from noonday clouds
anchored over a blue bay
to distant hills

Even the gentle sigh of waves
have reached for the deep breath of content
that marks the course of timelessness
with the colour of forever

Albert W.J. Harper

Summoned

A divine whisper
Of relief ...
Or would it be regret?
At having to meet
The challenges
Of this world.

He has summoned me
Not without
You wanting me
Not my name alone.

Waiting until
I can flourish
Unfolded in the flesh
Leaving go
The solitary shame
Of loneliness
In other worlds.

Never without
You calling me
Out of my absence
You reveal yourself
A priceless gift
For my trembling self
At the brink
Of my rebirth.

D. Hillen

Sounds In Silence

The silence here
articulates the swish of skis,
warns nature a visitor listens:

winds sound the air
announce their arrivals and departures,
as they move water in summer;

crows, heard, then seen
croak forward darkly,
a drone of deacons;

freshets shoosh under snow
here and there come up for air,
then laugh through the rocks at the shore;

lake-ice grinds its teeth
warns snowmobilers,
prepares for change;

jets, above the clouds, rumble
like computerized thunder,
recall deliberate sound:

the visitor listening
— a civilization needing —
sounds in silence.

Margaret Houben

Why Cat Eyes Glow In Dark

Curl up in sunny spot and snooze
Make like solar panel — absorb the sun
Sit in puddle of hot air and breathe deep
Pounce on light beams sneaking by
Catch every bit of light and heat by day
Then go out night-hunting with sunlit eyes

Sheila Hyland

Rustling Leaves/Birdsong

That fellow flogging the newspaper
Has the biggest ears I've ever seen
To look at them you'd think they'd
Be fine-tuned
But look again, see how he has
No use for them!

He cannot hear
His own cost calling
Coins jangling in his tin
Murmured "thanks" from buyers
Or voices of childern playing,
Traffic sounds are dumb and
Street musicians mimers

Oh those damned ears
The biggest pretenders
That will never hear
Rustling leaves/birdsong.

Susan Ioannou

Earth/Air

Earth to my air,
loam secret with fibre and root,

how could I not
be drawn from the wind

and trailing the seven moons of my being
wonder at your wet fragrance and darkness?

How could I not
kneel and dig for the sun glowing under,

dig and dig, needing to tumble
tendrilled, mossy, and soothed

out the upside-down sky
into a bolder noon?

How could you not
catch me falling through?

I.B. Iskov

upwards on windy stairs

i am like the mist
creeping softly
behind the hills
among cloud shadows
winding my way
home

the scorpion hustles
like the moon tides
slurring patterns
up and down
continuously
when the mood is right

i am changing
places quietly
on the cusp
between horizons
and seconds
come and go
without a place
to go

pushing upwards
like dust and debris
the scorpion
is worn down
little by little
struggling in shadows
on windy stairs

L. Johnson

Unsaid

The   spaces

     between

her   silences

were more

     profound

than any wisdom

passing discreetly   through

her lips.

And   I found myself

     listening

for wounded words

     unsaid.

Ernest Kapitany

The Door In The Mall

This door is permanent
it belongs to him
nobody dares to push him aside
it belongs to him
and his paper cup
which he holds in his palm lovingly

listen to shuffling shoes
whispering footsteps
coin drops
further cardboard figures
laugh from ads

the food court ignored all this

no payment guaranteed
he knows that
with this voluntary service
it is his entrepreneurship
his government created jobs

his lips move not for begging
not a signal nor a sound
he does not exist there

it's Ottawa or Toronto order
put him there without shame
why should he have any?

his car parked at the revenue building
in case
the minister wants a share

Zoë Kaszas

Flowing Ears

Noisy
sandpipers hovering above
the tide's impending
fullness,
as flourishing wavelets,
fluttering across,
meet
echolessly,
to consume the cringing
beach,
enfolding, motionless bare feet;
I let my voice
slip
into buoyant ears
of rhythmic listening.

Adèle Kearns Thomas

Almost Real

I fall incognito
into chasms of sleep
hide in ambushed light
these midnight trysts
of vague you and me
overshadowed
by the almost real
not standing still
mayhem
in uneasy sequences
span
distracted eyes
I can't keep pace
until jolt of wake-up.

Kathleen Kemp Haynes

The New Day

She had heard of the early a.m. shift
When morning would come sliding into view,
When tomorrow tumbled across the field
As fresh and beautiful as lawns in late spring.
She had been told that if you arose quite early
That the new day would appear before you
Ready-made and wonderful, as the old day
Disappeared on the far western horizon.
Chased by the demons which had already eaten
The promises and wishes made yesterday:
But if not alert in early morning's stupor,
You would miss the advent of the new day,
Never feel it slip over your shoulders and
Settle there briefly and defiantly brash.
Only weep for yesterday after morning
Has formally appeared on the freeze-frame of life.
One frame on the film of time is the old —
The next frame reveals the new, fully formed.
Who saw the switch? Hello, here is tomorrow!

Mohammad H. Khan

Vision

Tonight as I stroll down the street
   desert-lonely, yet brightly lit
I feel a strange, northern breeze
   blowing in endless streams.
O how it cools the heat of day
   fanning away my deep anxiety.
Its soft music soothing, refreshing.
   The secretion of fears has slowly disappeared
and life is beautiful!
   I gaze fixedly at the daisies bright with yellow,
whispering a friendly hello.
   The dew-sparkled petals tremble with bliss
by the glory of the moon kissed!
   Like ice upon scorching stone the anguish has gently
melted and how I am throbbingly elated with hope!
   At the sudden pitch of a star
tearing through the night
   sowed with countless seeds of light
my heart jumps, my spirit triumphs.
   My lips quiver a silent wish
for the reality of a vision.
   Waiting, secretly anticipating
my being expands with happiness!

Gary Kreller

Untitled

speak the words, say the phrases
stack them one
on one on
one
like plates to serve and bowls to drink
unmatched and chipped, oddly t
                i
              l
                  t
                e
             d
a leaning tower of sifted wisdom
eccentric circles of bits of fact
wash the dishes and clean the cups
passed from hand
to hand to
hand
like thoughts to share, lines to remember
borrowed and stolen, brightly painted
a polished thought of homespun china
spinning
balanced on a
s
t
i
c
k

Cecil Justin Lam

Forget Every Poem

If this would be
My best poem
I'd have to regress in time

Forget every poem
And chart a new course
Invoking the moon and the stars

Inspiration would
Whirl me back fast
And in a poetic fever

I'd draw you a portrait
So vivid and clear
So bright and so tight

You'd say
"Now that's a dramatic
Portrayal"

Carl A. Lapp

Will Power

Auntie, eighty-four,
jogs, drinks herbal tea,
takes Vitamin C and CoEnzymeQ$_{10}$

and has investments
ready to make millions
in the new millennium.

I send her a dozen altruistic roses every week.

Joan Latchford

In the Garden of the Church of St. George the Martyr

Sipping our coffee today
we watch summer's leaves play ring-around-a-rosie
(husha, husha, they all fall down)
turn cartwheels, over the still-green grass
with a dry rustle like taffeta.

We sit in the hidden garden
surrounded by lingering birdsong;
nursing the unnecessary warmth of our cups
to prolong these moments of random communication.

It would be enough,
Even if there is frost tonight and we argue tomorrow —
it would still be enough that you put your arm
around me as I lean against you
this perfect afternoon.

John B. Lee

The Curmudgeon's Apprentice

I am on the verge
of an expert disgruntlement.
I have perfected the deep twelve-toned harrumphs
of the river hippo.
I whisper epithets and imprecations
beneath the breath of love.
As it is with disappointed priests
and disapproving vicars, I moralize
my voice, low and lugubrious
as a parlour gramophone
dying in a groove.
I have managed the bitterness
of old tea
the dark tarnish of unattended silver
and the waxy orange match ends
of farmers
ruttling their ears in the evening.
I am living
at the existential rags' end
of all arguments.
I share a pessimism with the newly dead.
I practice hurling stones
at the dogs of the heart
to see them fly like barking birds
to hear them on the wind
howling above my words.

Monika Lee

Indwelling

Intend no other aim than silence
(so hard and worthy a plan)
bone simple.

To hold still inside a bubble
to let water surround a corpus floating,
do not steal the breath of indwelling
or the sparse glow of peace.

But be the bright and tranquil yolk
inside an egg,
or a birch leaf wayward floating
on a languid oval pond.

Pattern only the still droplet
in a cool cistern,
empty tankard
or stolen chalice.

For if a moment could be garnered
strange would be the lull.

Bernice Lever

Advice

And what have I to give?
just a list of my failures
slammed in my face doors
or snickering rejections
or plain icicle silences
    freezing my bravado retorts
of "I don't care."
when the whole block knows
I'm desperate for acceptance
    — just a hug to affirm
    I am worth touching —
but so often shunned as the leper
as others keep their gloves on
but still their claws cut
from across the crowded room.

How could I advise anyone about anything?
my life a non-model
so why try to second guess the fates
or ever question the heart,
for how can logic win
against this chaos called life?
percentages are no guarantee
for what worked for a thousand others
will surely fail for me
or if I suggest a path for you
the black trap will spring shut.

Melanie Lever

Baby Masks

At 5:00 a.m.
your wails can be heard

for farmyards,
just new whiskers
and baby tusk teeth
appear on my pillow,

guzzle back
goat's milk
faster than superman,

your tiny claws
wrapped, tighter 'round
my heart
than the bottle

John Loomis

Ablutions Of Time

A companion
of sixteen special years
died this winter.

Grief like a surfer's wave
slapped us into drunkards
cursing remembrances
far too pleasant,
hating our home
where her spirit lingered.

Sorrow washed over us
in a flood of panic
drowning senses,
unable to hear her voice
see her face
recall her joy.

Sadness slowly receded
born of acceptance,
memoried grains of sand
on separation's shore
began to dry
in the warmth of spring.

Laughter
sent by healing spirits
now rolls in
and we remember love
delivered with gusto
by a wagging tail.

Maynard Luterman

My Father's Reflection

what we are looking for
is who is looking
I lost it in what I thought
was my father's reflection
now I search for it
in yours

early morning on the lake
the glass-like surface
hides a world below
reflecting only what
I want to see
masking what I
choose to hide from

I trust mistrust
I am afraid
the truth
will destroy me

the gull circles   it knows
wings tucked it plummets
the silence is shattered
as it strikes the mirror
disappearing below
my reflection

mouth full
hunger gone
it reappears

the gull knows

Alice Major

III. Bilateral Symmetry

Dance floor   someone's wedding
and the deejay spinning a slow, remembered tune
— music coiling off the cassette
like double-sided tape peeled from its backing

we press
front to front
fingertip to fingertip
our hands
coupled
left for right
right for left
limb for limb we mirror
match

I glance up — your mouth
is tucked around a half-smile
we are equally
amused
by our languorous
twin   lust

but the heart is an asymmetric system —
blood flows in one
direction only   forced
by the squeeze of muscle through
the forked arteries   caught
and held again in the heart's
right chamber

I love you
I murmur in your ear
to keep the beat

Giovanni Malito

A Mother and Son Day

It was a conscious attempt
to write a history of my own.
I had planned to remember
you and me together
shopping for Paolo's gift
for his confirmation.
I had foreseen us roaming
through ages in the museum,
eating the decadent cakes
and drinking cappuccino
in the Yorkville café (already
a parking lot ... contemporary
history). It was to be our day
recorded in my own text,
a history never to collect dust
but only those few flakes of rust
that fall from an aging future.

Karen Massey

For the Stones in Her Pockets

> *This is death, death, death she noted in the margin*
> *of her mind; when illusion fails.*
> — Virginia Woolf, *Between the Acts*

fragile words are the woman
delicate inside her body
holding its secret captive over fifty years
filling her head with the wet sand of madness
she cannot climb out of its night
will not turn down the thick blankets of grief

like thrush eggs smooth inside her dress pockets
she carries brown speckled stones
to counteract the water's buoyancy
the stones are growing
are swelling with her life's heaviness
soon they burst the pocket seams
of her underwater skin

Virginia drowning off-stage like Ophelia
the silent weight of stone
drawing her down to muddy death
through decades of brilliant testimony
caught fluttering in pages

giant stones deliver her

A. McCormick

Dear Friend

Sweet wrinkled face
I have a special place for you
upon a pedestal
wearing a crown of pearls
and jade

Benevolent mistress
with spark
we laugh together
hug
share furies and philosophies
not often compatible

Moments cherished
spaced evenly upon
the blanket of time
wary of dissolving layers
that separate
and protect

Were it not for different eras
might we have despised each other?
Instead
respectful of the pedestal
the frailty of veils —

What's this?
Betrayer!
You crumple to the ground
resentful of youth
a mass of old bones and skin
barking wildly.

Hilton McCully (filidh na choille)

Air A'mhonadh

Bha mi air a'mhonadh an dé,
As morning sun made bright my day.
I marvelled at all the flowers of May,
When bha mi air a'mhonadh an dé.

A chirping frog beside the swamp,
Began his early morning romp.
By tinkling allt, the timid hare,
Hopped happily home to his cozy lair.
The morning thrush piped forth his lay,
A sprightly song to greet the day.
All Nature, it seemed, urged me to stay,
When bha mi air a'mhonadh an dé.

A stately stag, down by the burn,
Raised antlered head, from out the fern.
And these were the sights and sounds of May,
When bha mi air a'mhonadh an dé.

Explanations:
allt (pronounced "owlt") means "brook"
Bha mi air a'mhonadh an de (pronounced "Va me air uh vonnig un jay") means "I was on the moorland yesterday"

Joan McGuire

Grackle

Brash bird
raucous   obtrusive
    unadorned black
you squawk and flap
    goldfinches
and redpolls scatter
        yet now
you lie quiet
          dead
touched by a glint of sunlight
a subtle rainbow
       blue-green
          iridescent
shading into violet
and copper bronze

    all day
your agitated mate hops
around your broken body
such fidelity and caring in
a species so boisterous
as unexpected as the
lights revealing
your dark feathers hid
shimmering emerald and gold

Estelle McLachlan

Backsliding

If I should don my long and green-sleeved gown again
sometime, forgetting
and fall to my knees, suppliant before you
would you notice or, having forgotten also
merely see me as part and sad parcel
of your inventory of belongings?

If I repair to your burnished kitchens
meek at your command
present myself soon, chattel, neat of apron
bearing succulent dishes
lingering behind you at table
silent yet eager
for your cavalier word of approval;

if my eyes become downcast
my voice softly entreating
having sinned in your eyes
dwelt alone on the rack of guilt
for many days in my partitioned chamber;

if I come to you for your condescending forgiveness
for your speech returning me
to my bitter place
in your medieval kingdom, man's domain
bend to you, having backslid
my eloquent shoulders waiting;

then might you lean forward
sometime, remembering
and lift me, with sudden enlightenment
                         back
            into
      today?

Jill Meriel Fox

No Fixed Address

Huddled beside restaurant's
exhaust fan
he breathes in coffee, bacon
cinnamon buns
    exhales icicles into
his beard
    pees through layers
of Sally Ann second-hands
and mouldy sleeping bag
welcoming temporary warmth

Closing bloodshot eyes
he cannot
    will not see   beyond
this moment
this place
of no fixed address

The acrid taste of poverty
rises in his throat
choking
the crisp freshness of sheets
the soapy womb of bath water
the sated heaviness of second
helpings

He spits phlegm
        blood
        booze
to clear his memory

Hope Morritt

the talisman

i found your watch today
tucked into a dark corner
of the dresser drawer — a talisman
for me to wear like a charm
luring memories —
you spotlighted on stage
thanking the president
of the company for the
gold piece — twenty years
of safe driving through
sleet & rain & snow drifts
a canvas of lonely miles
now all gone —

i hold the talisman
in my warm palm
& feel your presence
sharply defined

Ben Murray

Ripe

what if all those
secret words
suffer soundlessly
in the close-packed dark
of their unopening?

piled in
perpetual readiness,
spines on shameless
beckoning display;

perhaps the occasional
flip-through, the periodic
cover-scan,
are reassurance
and reinforcement enough

that one day
the random chaos
of invisible ink
will be rendered
magically visible

by serene,
consuming eyes.

danieL peteR

Church Words

in the church of lost souls
a prayer for
mistakes they said
they'd make
praying not knowing the
words rather
believin' in fairy tales
being more sense to live by
o lordi the things you
make us do by and by
got to pretend we're talkin' to you
cause we're being watched
"don't ya know?"
praisin' the lord

Ted Plantos

Days of Numbered Pages

Winter is warm beside the stove
with my grandpappy singing

                Snow ignites the earth,
        and black is the soil of stripped-down hills

His songs of the fishermen, the sea,
go howling with the wind
and my eyes that follow
                the snowflakes down,
my eyes all lit up
with wondering about the sky
and how it changes colours

           Days of numbered pages curl
               into one another,
        and like the leaves that vanish,
       taking their portion of daylight
       to soft extinction in the ground,
I am counted away
with an earth that was his furious tongue

Anna Plesums

Holiday Echo

I flew back in time (half a century).
Childhood memories —
I had not learned about politics then.
     Politics do destroy —
     some things, some time, some where.
I saw footsteps of history:
remains of different cultures,
magnificent buildings and artworks
several centuries old.
But decades of communism
has left shadows and destruction,
shadows of ghettos,
shadows of gulags,
echoes of burning souls ...
     red — red — red ...
Blood mixed with vodka ...
Crime - a way of living.
Humanity — a foreign word ...
       Once upon a time I loved that country ...
    Canada — thanks for having me —
    Paradise could not be better ...

Wayne Ray

Gasping For Air

If I held you close,
placed my hands around
your ravens-wing hair
and pulled your face
into my chest so that
as you held your breath
and opened your bright eyes
you would gaze upon a map,
and in the upper corner
would be an image of you
standing naked on a pedestal
and all the roads on my
map of the human heart would
lead directly to you.
At this moment when we are one
in my embrace, you have the right
to take this image from
my heart wall or leave it there.
Either way, the memory of your
beauty remains and you pull back
from my flesh and hair, gasping for air.

Brian Rigg

In Dark June
for my friend Ray

seeing the sign on my way to school:
Hockey Players/Teams Needed!
I'm reminded of you
like a cold stone fist in the stomach
on this morning, your death is close again

thinking of a picture at nine
all long legs wrapped in foam
white-blond hair and big hands
bulging eyes behind those thick lenses
looking scared and really
only playing that sport because
everyone else wanted you to

you lying in that soft red space
          at the viewing
and one last time feeling
that I must touch your skin,
that your death
is so organized and already vague.
and how you loved Fridays; the song,
our game, the true passion time
when we played together

I'm hard against the night you died
that wicked bullet weaving its way
into your chest,
some minutes after I talked to you

in dark June it was graceless
your life unraveled
some time in the night, you died alone

Elizabeth Robitaille

Incommunicado

I have written you the most passionate letter.
Real Napoleon and Josephine stuff. On the thirteenth
reading, I grew frightened.

I made love to you with my words. I employed
vowels that slid like tongues over hollows and folds.
Consonants writhed like legs in damp sheets.

If you knew I loved you this way,
you would cower like the cornered dog you are. You'd fear
to look me in the eye. What burns there might blind you.

The letter had a pulse. Throbbed with muscle and purpose.
I could not bring myself to fold it, afraid I'd snap
its exquisite milk-fed bones.

On the third day, I wept as I tore the letter to shreds.
It succumbed.
        Not willingly.

When you return I will say, "How very nice to see you.
Did you have a pleasant holiday?"

Paul Sanderson

Guitarist

Guitarist warrior
holy man
the stage
a battlefront
audience anointed
by music
plunging like arrows
soul healing
catharsis
in electric church

Margaret Saunders

New Graveyard Over The Old Mine

Where coal-dusted miners
once surfaced, blinked daylight,
a sprawling new graveyard.

(The wind blew through
the warning whistle,
summoned a silent vigil,
the closing down
of number two.)

Somehow this green graveyard
with its fresh flowers
and shiny headstones
(although none of them
dedicated to you)
seems a fitting place,
a respectable resting place,
for you
who never made it
to the lighter side of day;
whose bones
still trapped in the earth's bowels,
lie beneath
the kindred souls
who lie beneath
these shiny stones.

Jeff Seffinga

The Winter Horses

No mist lies on the distant hills
and mountains. In the ice clear air
only a straight string of smoke rises.
Behind the barn steam dissipates
in thin wisps from the fresh manure.
Two horses stand in a private heat
that lies almost solid along
the backs and haunches. Their breath comes
in quiet little white clouds puffing
from dark nostrils. They stand so calm
in the cold with no wind tugging at
their manes and tails, eyes almost closed
against the frost. Heads down, they don't
doze. They wait for the grain and water,
for fresh straw on the floor. Small dreams
of summer fields shiver under their hides
with traces of longing but no regrets.
A door opens. They return to warm stalls.

K.V. Skene

Under Glass
(*The Book of Kells*)

Under museum-light saints, angels,
all the companies of heaven appear
in cloth of gold, ruby, sapphire, emerald,
amber. Lurking, lies a gilt
and grinning wolf, sly rabbit, curious
cat, bejewelled bird — strange
and soulful creature-symbols scribed
on fine, flesh-scraped, lime-bleached
vellum. The Gospels (Latin text
copied more than a thousand years ago)
illuminated for the illiterate
by inspired Irish monks. For love
of God, for His glory — or
for the hell of it.

Raymond Souster

By The Day Of The Election

By the day of the election
I'd become so depressed,
I went out and voted
For our local liberal candidate.

Brenda Spearing

Doppelganger
for Robert Sward

Am i going crazy?
Or is it You again?
Appearing in a different suit.

Not denim, cambray or harris tweed.
Leather,
Soft leather, sun-tanned, pungent, body-warm
Leather.
Lovingly aged by time and wrinkles,
Wintered by wives, children and lives.
Too many lives; too many wives.
Beginnings, endings, repetitious renderings
Of unrequited Love.

Not a simple task is it?
This looking for God.
Are you as tired as i am?

Darlene Spong Henderson

Café

She sat at the corner table
sipping her latte
bright sunlight
enrobing her Armani suit.
Glancing at her Rolex
her annoyance was visible.
Her lunch date was late.

Perfectly manicured fingernails
tapped the table's cold marble surface.

It appeared that she was
staring
at the pregnant street resident
who stood at the gutter
plastic and cardboard
wrapped around her swollen feet;
matted hair groping at her dirt-streaked face;
desolation and despair
her aura.

But the lady by the window
whose lunch date was late
saw nothing
but her own rage.

Gerry Stewart

Glenco

The eye is silent
as we imagine the storm. The wind masking
the blood-axe blow
on bone, the dying screams, the rush of
blood-sluiced stream.

Sacrificed for greed
and gold the memory of the fallen fades.
Sepia faces
forgotten, names transformed to fiction, the
bile of ancient myths.

Infused with fear, flesh
and bone the moaning wind above the knoll
echos the pain of
earth-bound souls soaked in blood-stained soil
alone, forever.

Elizabeth St Jacques

In Prayer
(haiku sequence)

April moon ...
on return from evening prayers
the young nun sighs

hands
inside her sleeves again —
the old nun's habit

convent grounds ...
the starward gaze
of that stone virgin

Isabel Sturgeon

Forest Fancy

There's a lovelight in the forest
      when the maples drop their leaves,
A golden carpet for rabbits
      for fluffy tails to play on;
Comes the sound of a gun shot
      now there's blood drops on my shoe!

This poem is a Sijo — Korean-style poetry in English.

Lynn Tait

American Gothic

A portrait of a sterile existence
a study of two sore thumbs
      stiffly sticking to barren rules.
Can see
      the children leave
unable to face Mother's eyes
      ironed on displeasure
      worn like starched sheets
unable to crack Father's glacial crust
      an inland ingrained
      with empty furrows.
Locked in a fist
      life spark clenches farm weapons
      sharp as tongue lashings,
pierces land unyielding as his heart.

Left to weather elements alone
      offspring take root in cities
      steel and concrete
      give way to forgiving flesh,
show of teeth
      something other than a sneer,
      ideas allowed to expand,
      room made for color,
hearts without fear,
      without the devil and his pitchfork
      bloodying up the landscape.

Stephen Threlkeld

O.R.

Six priests fish
Around a small pool
As the aromatic air
Of the silvery woods,
Where April bluebells
Toxically grow,
Fills with strange images:
Butterflies,
As large as plates,
A girl with a crown
Of peppermint leaves
And anklets of basil,
Dances in a gossamer shift
To the music of
A didgeridu
From another land,
Played by a little boy
Dressed like the boy in blue,
As a winged white horse
Crosses my path.
At last, full of peace
I surrender,
And, comfortable
On pine needles
Of red and gold,
I slowly fall asleep.

Heather Tisdale-Nisbet

Railway Hotel

The passenger trains only stop at this station
twice a day now and
never in the evening.

The railway hotel went to
a big chain in a sweet deal
and they abandoned it.

The sign says it's closed for renovations,
but there's been no work here for a year.

The rooms still have blinds
or drapes in the windows,
the red brick gleams in the sun;
if you peer through the glass
to the lobby
you can see litter,
as if everyone left quickly
and threw their cigarette butts on the carpet
in disgust.

So there's no wandering
in the train station now
and there's no sauntering
through the hotel lobby;
the money went offshore
and left an empty honeycomb.

M. Mickey Turnbull

United in a Danse Macabre

There's no escape but still I flee,
Through black of night in misery,
In flowing nightgown, midnight shroud,
Bare feet across the dew-damp ground,
No hiding place to set me free
From Spectre Pain who captures me
With cruel intent, he holds me fast,
United in Macabre Danse.

Captured, entrapped, beyond despair,
The shadow of pain is everywhere ...
I fast lose ground to this black fiend
Who thirsts for power o'er my being,
Together, Yin and Yang locked fast,
United in Macabre Danse.

I cry aloud ... please set me free,
There's more to life than agony,
I'll live with pain but give me space,
Please free me from this dark embrace
This misery can't be all I have,
United in a Danse Macabre.

Frances Ward-Marciniak

a poet walked by

not long ago
i opened the blinds
     early evening
     winter darkness

a poet was walking by

i know he's a poet
he knows he's a poet

nobody else does

he looked up
startled by my
backlit form

i closed the blinds

he has bigger things
to write about

Ida-May Wegner

Friendship

It's overwhelming how in chance our souls have met,
Touching my life with your kindness,
It's that compassion,
That compels one to the other,
And has become our common bond.

Together our spirits were connected by an unseen force,
Which has the potential to transform mere strangers into friends,
In this attraction we have grown,
To respect each other's individual desires,
Preserving and enhancing this precious gift of friendship.

So sacred is this act of giving,
And with this devotion we have shown,
A depth and passion without limits,
Where all can be unspoken,
And understood.

Honored at how profusely you give of yourself,
Asking nothing in return,
And always you are there.

Norma West Linder

Parsons Street Poet

Carmen is drawn to flowers
as flies to cookie crumbs and
hiker's feet to nature trails
She is always the one to spot
Jack-in-the-pulpit's green spear
through the forest floor.

So it is only fitting
that of all the cherry trees
lining her street
the one facing her house
each year is first to burst
into pink blossoms.

She revels in the riches
of every lower limb
the way a true gourmet
savours a meal
the way a mother sees
her first born smile.

Richard Woollatt

Thirty-Six Pelicans

Thirty-six pelicans all in a row

gliding

      single file

parallel to beach

like a long gold chain

        finely meshed

skimming over palms

in majestic

      mute precision

above a welter of obese

grotesque

      sunburnt humans

Michael Wurster

Oubliette

He carried his gift up the three steps
to the rented canoe. He could live
with mother's dying, dead, he said.

The poplar leaves whispered;
the maker's initials were engraved
on the gift, and the inscription:

"Out of want, Out of darkness." A seed
on the tongue. "I missed you when I came
to visit." "Why didn't you just phone?"

Memory resurrects no one. What a joke.
A canoe, then a bus. Clichés make it
no better. The tears formed, the fish

were eaten. Plainsong, call and response.
I laughed my head off as he disappeared
around the bend of the river.

Carmen Ziolkowski

Swan Song

I have travelled the circle
wearing all my dresses
the cherry blossom
and strawberry red of spring
velvety green and burned gold
sprinkled
with the dust of summer
when the sky was blue
and starved for cloud —

With a flourish
I flaunted the brightest colours
olive branch silver
bright red and yellow
when the rusty leaves were falling
wearing contrapuntal melodies —

Now this cosmic planet turning grey
my dresses are in tatters
creatures scamper under branches
dancing a whirlwind
searching for acorn or chestnut —
and I in my white bones

Afterword

On the afternoon of February 24, 1985, ten or so people had the first official Canadian Poetry Association meeting. It was decided to have a Board of Directors and Bev Duario, Shaunt Basmajian, Ted Plantos and Wayne Ray were elected.

On March 5, 1985, Shaunt Basmajian wrote a letter — "TO ALL MEMBERS: A Brief Note:" It was agreed the main objective would be to promote a broader exposure of poetry to the general public and hopefully develop into an international connection for Canadian poets. We also agreed we would work in harmony with other groups and organizations and include both poets and poetizers alike in the organization. A note on the founding of the organization was written and typed up by Chris Faiers a few days later and mailed to those that seemed interested.

The CPA aims to promote the reading, writing, publishing and preservation of poetry in Canada through the individual efforts of members; to promote communication amongst poets, publishers and the general public; to encourage leadership and participation from members and to encourage the formation and development of autonomous local chapters.

Membership in the Canadian Poetry Association is open to anyone with an interest in poetry, including non-poets and members of other literary organizations. The CPA is a member-driven and a member-controlled organization. It is a group of people interested in poetry moreso than in the poets.

This anthology reflects our membership. Very disparate poets and very individual poetry. The only criteria for inclusion in *Strong Winds* is membership in CPA. This, I believe, is the charm: the difference, its non-judgmental structure and its openness.

The *Strong Winds* Committee of Judith Anderson Stuart, Alan Briesmaster, Sheila Hyland and Ted Plantos did a solid job of managing this project, with Sheila Hyland doing a detailed and imaginative job of the editing. They are all volunteers and we thank them for their efforts.

— Jennifer Footman, President
Canadian Poetry Association
June 1997

Canadian Poetry Association

The Canadian Poetry Association was founded in 1985 to promote all aspects of the writing, reading, publishing, purchasing, performing and preservation of poetry in Canada. Nationally, the CPA publishes the bimonthly *Poemata* newsletter, coordinates member poetry anthologies—*An Invisible Accordion* (1995) and *Strong Winds* (1997)—and other publications and activities.

The Canadian Poetry Association promotes the creation of local chapters everywhere in Canada. Local chapters often organize readings, workshops, publishing projects, readings and other poetry-related events in their area. Local chapters are in Parry Sound, London, Toronto, Sarnia, the Maritimes, Guelph, Hamilton and Brampton.

The lifeline of the CPA, *Poemata* features news articles, chapter reports, poetry by new members, book reviews, markets information, announcements and more.

The CPA inaugurated several projects in 1996: the Shaunt Basmajian Chapbook Award, the Canadian Poetry Association Poetry Chapbook Series, the Canadian Poetry Association Award for Contributions to Poetry, and Canadian Poetry Association Life Memberships. The CPA has also been instrumental in developing the Acorn-Livesay People's Festival.

Join the Canadian Poetry Association

Membership in the CPA is based upon the calendar year (1 January to 31 December). Membership includes a subscription to *Poemata*. Local chapters may have their own membership requirements and/or additional fees. You don't even have to be a poet to join. Publishers, schools, libraries, booksellers, and other friends of poetry are most welcome! Regular membership $30. Seniors and students $20.

For a membership form, or to join, please write to:
Canadian Poetry Association
BOX 22571 ST GEORGE PO
TORONTO ON M5S 1V0

Acknowledgements

The following poems in *Strong Winds* have been previously published. Winona Baker: portions of "Haiku Seasonal" in *Frogpond* and *Modern Haiku*. Joe Blades: "Mona Lévi" in a series of paintings with Dale McMullin, in *Sapodilla*, and broadcast on *Ashes, Paper & Beans* (CHSR). Evelyn Broy: "A Woman's Cheek" in *The Noblest Frailty* (Cranberry Press). Caroline H. Davidson: "Neighbours" in *Uncivilizing* (Insomniac Press). James Deahl: "Prayer for the Dead In September" in *Chapman* (Scotland). Sonja Dunn: "Ukraine Poem 1" in *Spring Fever: Writes of Spring '97* (Your Scrivener Press). Bernadette Dyer: "Stone Woman" in *Jones Av.* Raymond Fenech : "Life Passes You By" in *Point of No Return* (Poetry Now Publishers, UK). Kathy Fretwell: "Summer Hiatus" in *Quarry*. Edward Gates: "XXV" in *The Fiddlehead*. Katherine L. Gordon: "Night of the Wolves" in *Writual*. I.B. Iskov: "upwards on windy stairs" in *Outreach Connection*. John B. Lee: "The Curmudgeon's Apprentice" in *The Sandwich Mill Anthology* (Cranberry Tree Press) and *Never Hand Me Anything If I Am Walking Or Stand* (Black Moss Press). Monika Lee: "Indwelling" in *Poets' Podium*. Bernice Lever: "Advice" in *Mix Six* (Mekler & Deahl, Publishers). Alice Major: "III. Bilateral Symmetry" in *Whetstone*. Karen Massey: "For The Stones In Her Pockets" in *G.L.I.B.* Hilton McCully: "Air A'mhonadh" in *N.S. Retired Teacher*. Anna Plesums: "Holiday Echo" in *The Best Poems of 1997* (National Library of Poets, USA). Elizabeth Robitaille: "Incommunicado" in *The Wicked*. Margaret Saunders: "New Graveyard Over The Old Mine" in *Bridging the Gap* (Moonstone Press) and on WTN (Women's Television Network). Gerry Stewart: "Glenco" is forthcoming on a Sax Appeal CD in 1998. Elizabeth St Jacques: "In Prayer" in part in *HWUP! Poetry Newsletter* and in *Dance of Light* (Maplebud Press). Lynn Tait: "American Gothic" in *Seeds* e-zine. M. Mickey Turnbull: "United In A Danse Macabre" in *Reflections By Moonlight* (Poetry Institute of Canada). Ida-May Wegner: "Friendship" forthcoming in *Whispers from the Soul* (Plowman Press).

The Contributors

Becky Alexander resides in Preston, ON. She has been published in *The Toronto Sun*, *Guideposts*, *Kindred Spirits*, *Country Woman*, *Canadian Author*, and other periodicals.

Claire Alexander finds fulfillment in teaching ESL to beginner-level adult immigrants. She and her husband, Harold, live on a Quarter Horse farm in King City.

Judith Anderson Stuart avenges herself on her partner and their sons — literally. A graduate of University of Toronto, she is in doctoral studies at York University.

Beryl Baigent is a teacher of Tai Chi, Yoga, and dance. She is the author of nine poetry books, most recently: *Triptych: Virgin Victims Votives* (Moonstone).

Winona Baker is the International Winner in the 1989 Basho Haiku Contest. She has four collections of poetry published.

George I. Bernstein practices orthopaedic surgery in Windsor, Ontario. His stories, poems, essays, and book reviews appear in Canadian and American journals. He is a contributing editor for *Mediphors*.

German-born Jack Baum settled in Canada in 1956. He has authored six booklets in English and five in German. His poems appear nationally and internationally.

Joe Blades lives in New Brunswick. His publications include *Tribeca* (above/ground press) and a nonfiction book, *In The Dark—Poets & Publishing* (Broken Jaw Press).

Allan Briesmaster is the National Co-ordinator of the Canadian Poetry Assiciation. His poetry is in *Mix Six* (Mekler & Deahl and *Understatement* (Seraphim Editions).

Linda M. Brissett is a Registered Nurse/Midwife. The author of three poetry books and a book of short stories, she has contributed to *Ingots* and *The First Time*.

Evelyn J. Broy, born in England, has lived about half her life in Glasgow, Scotland and half in Ontario. Her poetry book *Almanac of Absence* was published in 1996.

Mary Chryssoulakis who was born in Montreal, has lived in Sarnia for 40 years. She has been publishing her work in little magazines and anthologies since 1967.

Barbara Coulston lives and works in Toronto as a pharmacist. She enjoys such creative pursuits as: singing, writing, and acting. She is a new member of the CPA.

Dina Cox, former high school teacher, is a musician and mother of four. She explores her poetic capabilities through reading and writing poetry.

Caroline H. Davidson, born in Ithica, NY, lives in Pickering. Writing since high school, her work has appeared in newspapers and anthologies.

James Deahl is a past president of the CPA. He currently edits *Poemata*. His most recent book is *Under The Watchful Eye* (Broken Jaw Press).

Luci Dilkus is a native of Toronto, a York University graduate, a conceptual/installation artist and a writer of poetry.

Sonja Dunn has written ten books for children. She is an author, drama consultant, storyteller, poet, performer, actor, t.v. producer and language arts specialist.

Bernadette Dyer is a poet, storyteller, playwright, illustrator and short story writer who lives in Toronto.

Bob Ezergailis writes poetry, sculpts, is a painter and photographer. He has published *The Thoughts of the Last Futurist*, and "The Morphealist Manifesto".

Raymond Fenech has worked as a freelancer with major political newspapers. Born in Malta, he has published in Malta, Italy, UK, USA, Canada and Argentina.

Penny Ferguson's poetry book, *Runaway Suite: Two Voices*, is published by Hidden Brook Press. She is also editor of *The Amethyst Review* in Truro, Nova Scotia.

Peggy Fletcher, born in St. John's, Newfoundland, a former editor of the *Sarnia Observer*, *Canadian Poetry* and *Mamashee*, has published four books of poetry.

Jennifer Footman, Brampton, Ontario poet, is Chair of the Canadian Poetry Association, and author of three poetry books including *St Valentine's Day*.

Linda Frank, born in Montreal, lives in Hamilton, Ontario. Her poems have appeared in several Canadian journals and in the chapbook, *Taste The Silence*.

Kathy Fretwell published two books with Fiddlehead Poetry Books and has poems in 11 anthologies including *Mix Six* and *The Dry Wells of India*.

Edward Gates is a blueberry farmer in Belleisle Creek, NB. "XXV" is from *Seeing The World With One Eye*, a forthcoming ghazal collection with Broken Jaw Press.

Ben Genereaux was in 1968 in Belleville, Ontario. Currently on the road, Ben has three chapbooks in the works for later this year. This is his first publication.

Katherine L. Gordon is a rural poet, book reviewer and editor contributing regularly to anthologies in the US and Canada. She also heads the CPA chaper in Guelph.

Richard M. Grove is a Toronto artist, writer and editor/publisher of a paper- and web site-based poetry zine called *Seeds*. His work appears in various publications.

Albert W.J. Harper, a retired resident of London, Ontario, has published two poetry books. His work has also appeared in philosophical journals in Canada and abroad.

D. Hillen lives in the very centre of Hamilton. He writes poetry and opinion pieces on education, in the main.

Margaret Houben was born in, and lives in B.C. She has published poems in anthologies and in one chapbook.

Sheila Hyland writes poetry and prose and has published four collections of poetry.

Susan Ioannou is author of *Clarity Between Clouds* (Goose Lane) and *Where The Light Waits* (Ekstasis Editions), and is founder/director of Wordwrights Canada.

I.B. (Bunny) Iskov has published her poetry in numerous periodicals and anthologies. Her third chapbook is coming out in the CPA Poetry Series.

L. Johnson is a co-ordinator of a new Rogers Cable poetry program *Millennial Wave* and editor/publisher of Holland Landing Writers' Group's *Write Outside the Lines*.

Ennest Kapintany came to Canada in 1957 from Budapest, Hungary and worked in the Montreal fashion industry. His poetry has been published in newspapers, etc.

Zoë Kaszas lives in Kitchener, Ontario. She is a sculptor of hand-built clay figures as well as a poet. Her poetry has been published in *Poets' Podium* and *Companions*.

Adèle Kearns Thomas, originally from Quebec, now resides in Sarnia. She has published one book of poetry: *Behind The Scenes*.

Kathleen Kemp Haynes is a grandmother who lives and writes in Dorchester, a Southern Ontario village. She is a graduate of the University of Western Ontario.

Mohammad Khan's hometown, Wismar, British Guiana was destroyed during the civil war and his eldest brother was murdered. He fled Guyana for Canada in 1983.

Gary Kreller is a published writer and musician. He is currently working on a novel and a collection of performance pieces combining music and poetry.

Carl A. Lapp is a US born London, Ontario psychiatrist and father of three children. His poems have been in *White Wall Review* and the *Naked Physician* anthology.

Joan Latchford was born in 1926. Her photos have appeared in books and poetry anthologies. Since 1993, her photographer's eye has found expression in words.

John B. Lee is a prolific writer who has won many awards for his poetry. His most recent book is *Tongues Of The Children* (Black Moss Press).

Monika Lee is a mother of two girls, a poet, and a professor of English at Brescia College in London.

Bernice Lever, of Richmond Hill, Ont., edited *Waves* for 15 years, teaches at Seneca College, co-ordinates the Richvale Writers Club and has authored 11 books.

Melanie Lever is currently inspired by the mountain peaks around Whistler, B.C.

John Loomis and his wife Susan run a music academy. John is a music critic and late-blooming poet who unwinds by riding horses over fences.

Dr. Maynard Luterman was born in Montreal. He did his studies at The Johns Hopkins University, Baltimore and McGill University, Montreal.

Alice Major is a freelance writer in Edmonton. Recently, she read at the University of Leeds, as a finalist in *Stand Magazine*'s international poetry competition.

Giovani Malito's first collection, *Touching The Moon* (Bradshaw Books), came out in June 1997. A second collection, *Animal Crackers* (Aramby), is forthcoming.

Karen Massey received her MA (Poetry) from Concordia and has worked as an artisan in Ottawa since 1990. Her poems appear in various literary publications.

Anne McCormick enjoys writing poetry, fiction and non-fiction.

Hilton McCully (filidh na choille) is a retired teacher in Dartmouth NS. He is the author of six publications. His work is also found in Canadian and US anthologies.

Joan Mcguire, a retired social worker, cycles, swims and cross-country skis. Her poetry has been published in *TickleAce, Zygote, Scrivener* and other publications.

Estelle McLachlan has published poetry and prose in Canada, USA and Australia. She has won six awards for poetry in Canadian contests since 1988.

Jill Meriel Fox says "when other relationships have attempted to define her: friend, lover, co-worker, wife, mother, teacher, it is poetry which takes her by the hand and reintroduces her to self."

Hope Morritt lives and writes in Sarnia, close to Lake Huron. Her published works include: *Soldier Come Home* and *Rivers Of Oil*. She is presently working on a novel.

Ben Murray, of Edmonton, when not cat walking or searching for affordable vegan fig bars, deliberates over becoming reincarnated as P.K. Page or Robert DeNiro.

danieL peteR was born and raised in Toronto where he presently lives with his wife and son. He teaches grade 7 at St. Lawrence School in Scarborough.

Ted Plantos has authored 11 poetry books and two children's books. Black Moss Press is publishing his new and selected poems, *Daybreak's Long Waking*, this fall.

Anna Plesums says: "her past is 73 years long. But there are no recipes how to grow old, so I wonder about tomorrow in poetry. Most of my days are sunny."

Wayne Ray, poet, author and publisher of HMS Press, maintains the CPA London website: http://www.MIRROR.org/groups/cpa and Listserv: cpa@wwdc.com

Lini Richarda Grol is a Canadian citizen from The Netherlands. A playwright, poet, and scissor-cut illustrator, her work has appeared widely in books and periodicals.

Brian Rigg attends York University and works with developmentally challenged individuals. He has been published in *Canadian Dimension, Fireweed* and *Propaganda*.

Elixabeth Robitaille lives, writes, and mothers four sons in Bright's Gove, Ontario.

Paul Sanderson, a Toronto arts lawyer and poet, has written two legal books: *Model Agreements for Visual Artists* (CARO) and *Musicians and the Law in Canada* (Carswell).

Margaret Saunders is the author of three chapbooks of haiku, one full-length book of poetry, and two books for children. She lives in Hamilton, Ontario.

Jeff Seffinga is the author of four poetry collections. He promotes poetry and related activities in Hamilton, Ontario.

K.V. Skene is a Canadian who's lived in Quebec, Ontario and B.C. In 1993, she moved to England. Her work has appeared in North American and UK publications.

Raymond Souster was born in Toronto in 1921 and employed with the CBIC from 1939-84. He has published 60 books — poetry, novels, and as an editor.

Brenda Spearing, of Richmond Hill and The Richvale Writers Group, is a part-time banker. She has enjoyed 22 years performing in amateur theatrical productions.

Darlene Spong Henderson, born and raised in London, Ontario, resides with her family in St. Albert, Alberta. She has published poetry in the *Edmonton Journal*.

Gerry Stewart is a Mississauga poet who spends most of his energy playing saxophone with his tio, Sax Appeal. They are working on a second CD for spring 1998 release.

Elizabeth St Jacques is the author of eight books of poetry including *A Dance of Light*, which won the Merit Book Award from Haiku Society of America.

Isabel Sturgeon, a Canadian and international award-winning artist, studied in Europe and the Yukon, and attended the Ottawa School of Art.

Lynn Tait lives in Sarnia with her husband, son and cat. She drives a school bus to support her writing habit. She has published poetry in Canada and the US.

Stephen Threlkeld grew up in Cornwall, England before moving to Canada, where he has spent most of his life. He is attracted to Taoist philosophy.

Heather Tisdale-Nisbet lives in Nepean, Ontario. Her poetry has appeared recently in *Poets' Podium* and *Jones Av*.

M. Mickey Turnbull was photojournalist with double by-lines in Aruba and has published in more than 30 anthologies and newsletters.

Frances Ward-Marciniak, born in England, came to Canada as a child. A poet and painter in Hamilton, she has published in *Kairos* and in *Ingots* anthology.

Ida-May Wegner is a wife and mother living in Hamilton, Ontario. She has been writing poetry most of her life and enjoys sharing it with others.

Norma West Linder, author of five novels, six poetry collections, a memoir, and a children's book, is past president of CAA Sarnia branch and a member of TWUC.

Richard Woollatt, a writer and former English teacher living in Burlington, Ontario, has poetry published in *Ingots*, a Hamilton sesquicentennial anthology.

Michael Wurster teaches at the Pittsburgh Centre for the Arts School in Pennsylvania. He has recent work appearing in *Poemata, 5 AM* and *Poet Lore*.

Carmen Ziolkowski's poetry has appeared in magazines in Italy, Canada, Australia, USA, and England. She is the author *Roses Bloom At Dusk*, and *World Of Dreams*.

A Selection Of Our Titles In Print

Title	ISBN	Price
96 Tears (in my jeans) (Vaughan)	0-921411-65-0	3.95
Anxiety Attack (Iskov)	0-921411-50-2	3.95
Best in Life (Mouradian)	0-921411-55-3	17.95
Best Lack All, The (Schmidt)	0-921411-37-5	12.95
Chaste Wood (Wendt)	0-921411-11-1	7.95
Cover Makes a Set (Blades)	0-919957-60-9	8.95
Cranmer (Hawkes)	0-921411-66-9	4.95
Crossroads Cant (Grace, et al)	0-921411-48-0	13.95
Danger Falling Ice (Blades (ed.)) BSPS	0-9694127-2-X	4.95
Dark Seasons (Trakl; Skelton (trans.))	0-921411-22-7	10.95
Earth Aches (Gibbs)	0-921411-36-7	2.95
Gift of Screws (Hannah)	0-921411-56-1	12.95
Hawthorn (Bull; Bull)	0-921411-24-3	4.95
In the Dark—Poets & Publishing (Blades)	0-921411-62-6	9.95
InCorrupt Tables, The (Vaughan)	0-921411-44-8	2.95
Invisible Accordion, An (Footman (ed.))	0-921411-38-3	14.95
Lad from Brantford, A (Richards)	0-921411-25-1	11.95
Luke and the Wolf (Bell) BSPS	0-9694127-3-8	4.95
Memories of Sandy Point (Pieroway, P)	0-921411-33-2	14.95
Only the Salt (Underhill)	0-921411-35-9	13.95
Open 24 Hours (Burke, et al)	0-921411-64-2	13.95
Poems from the Blue Horizon (mclennan)	0-921411-34-0	3.95
Poems for Little Cataraqui (Folsom)	0-921411-28-6	10.95
Milton Acorn Reading from More Poems for People. (C-45 cassette) (Acorn)	0-921411-63-4	9.95
Rum River (Fraser)	0-921411-61-8	16.95
Speak! (Larwill, et al)	0-921411-67-7	13.95
St Valentine's Day (Footman)	0-921411-45-6	13.95
Strong Winds (Hyland (ed.))	0-921411-60-X	14.95
There are No Limits to How Far the Traveller Can Go (Gates)	0-921411-54-5	4.95
This Grievous Injury (Hawkes)	0-921411-41-3	2.95
Under the Watchful Eye (Deahl)	0-921411-30-8	11.95
View from the Bucket, A (Redekopp)	0-921411-52-9	14.95
Voir Dire (Flaming)	0-921411-26-X	11.95

Ask your favourite bookseller to order these titles from **General Distribution Services**, 30 Lesmills Rd, Don Mills ON M3B 2T6. Telephone orders: Toronto 416 445-3333; Ontario/Quebec 1-800-387-0141; Atlantic and Western Canada 1-800-387-0172; USA 1-800-805-1083.

To order direct from the publisher, individual orders must be prepaid with cheque or money order. Please add $2 shipping for one book ($9.95 and up) and $0.50 per additional item. All Canadian orders must add 7% GST/HST.

MARITIMES ARTS PROJECTS PRODUCTIONS
BOX 506 STN A
FREDERICTON NB E3B 5A6   Ph/fax: 506 454-5127
CANADA   E-mail: jblades@nbnet.nb.ca